TO:
Jennifer,
David,
and Baby!

♡, Joanna & Patric

LITTLE SONGS OF LONG AGO

ILLUSTRATIONS BY
HENRIETTE WILLEBEEK LE MAIR
EDITED BY DAWN AND PETER COPE

GALLERY CHILDREN'S BOOKS
LONDON AND THE HAGUE

THIS VOLUME OF BEAUTIFULLY
ILLUSTRATED NURSERY RHYMES
IS THE WORK OF THE DUTCH ARTIST
HENRIETTE WILLEBEEK LE MAIR (1889-1966).

SHE WAS THE DAUGHTER OF A
WEALTHY MERCHANT WHO HAD AN INTEREST
IN ART AND ENCOURAGED HER TO PAINT AND
DRAW FROM AN EARLY AGE.

PUBLISHERS WERE ATTRACTED BY HER
DELICATE AND DETAILED DRAWINGS AND
HER FEELING FOR DECORATION AND
MISS LE MAIR WAS COMMISSIONED TO
ILLUSTRATE SEVERAL CHILDREN'S BOOKS
WITH RHYMES BETWEEN 1911-1926.

'LITTLE SONGS OF LONG AGO' FIRST PUBLISHED
IN 1912, AND ITS COMPANION VOLUME
'OUR OLD NURSERY RHYMES', 1911, ARE SURELY
THE MOST BEAUTIFUL SET OF ALL THE
BEST-LOVED RHYMES EVER ILLUSTRATED.

CONTENTS

Curly locks, Curly locks,
    Wilt thou be mine?
Thou shalt not wash dishes
    Nor yet feed the swine;
But sit on a cushion
    And sew a fine seam,
And feed upon strawberries,
    Sugar and cream.

5

Hickory, dickory, dock,
The mouse ran up the clock;
The clock struck one,
    The mouse ran down,
Hickory, dickory, dock.

Hickory, dickory, dare,
    The pig flew up in the air;
The man in brown
    Soon brought him down,
Hickory, dickory, dare.

Dame, get up and bake your pies,
    Bake your pies, bake your pies;
Dame, get up and bake your pies,
    On Christmas day in the morning.

Dame, what makes your maidens lie,
    Maidens lie, maidens lie;
Dame, what makes your maidens lie,
    On Christmas day in the morning?

Dame, what makes your ducks to die,
    Ducks to die, ducks to die;
Dame, what makes your ducks to die,
    On Christmas day in the morning?

Their wings are cut and they cannot fly,
    Cannot fly, cannot fly;
Their wings are cut and they cannot fly,
    On Christmas day in the morning.

Three mice went into a hole to spin;
Pussy passed by and she peeped in.
What are you doing, my little men?
Weaving coats for gentlemen.
Shall I come in and cut off your threads?
No, no, Mistress Pussy, you'd bite off our heads.
Oh, no, I'll not; I'll help you to spin.
That may be so, but you don't come in.

11

Here am I,
Little Jumping Joan;
When nobody's with me
I'm all alone.

13

Little Polly Flinders
Sat among the cinders,
Warming her pretty little toes;
    Her mother came and caught her,
And whipped her little daughter
For spoiling her nice new clothes.

Pat-a-cake, pat-a-cake, baker's man,
Bake me a cake as fast as you can;
Pat it and prick it, and mark it with B,
Put it in the oven for baby and me.

London Bridge is broken down,
   Broken down, broken down,
London Bridge is broken down,
   My fair lady.

Build it up with wood and clay,
   Wood and clay, wood and clay,
Build it up with wood and clay,
   My fair lady.

Wood and clay will wash away,
   Wash away, wash away,
Wood and clay will wash away,
   My fair lady.

Built it up with bricks and mortar,
   Bricks and mortar, bricks and mortar,
Build it up with bricks and mortar,
   My fair lady.

Bricks and mortar will not stay,
   Will not stay, will not stay,
Bricks and mortar will not stay,
   My fair lady.

Build it up with iron and steel,
   Iron and steel, iron and steel,
Build it up with iron and steel,
   My fair lady.

Iron and steel will bend and bow,
   Bend and bow, bend and bow,
Iron and steel will bend and bow,
   My fair lady.

Built it up with silver and gold,
   Silver and gold, silver and gold,
Build it up with silver and gold,
   My fair lady.

Silver and gold will be stolen away,
   Stolen away, stolen away,
Silver and gold will be stolen away,
   My fair lady.

Set a man to watch all night,
   Watch all night, watch all night,
Set a man to watch all night,
   My fair lady.

LITTLE TOMMY TUCKER

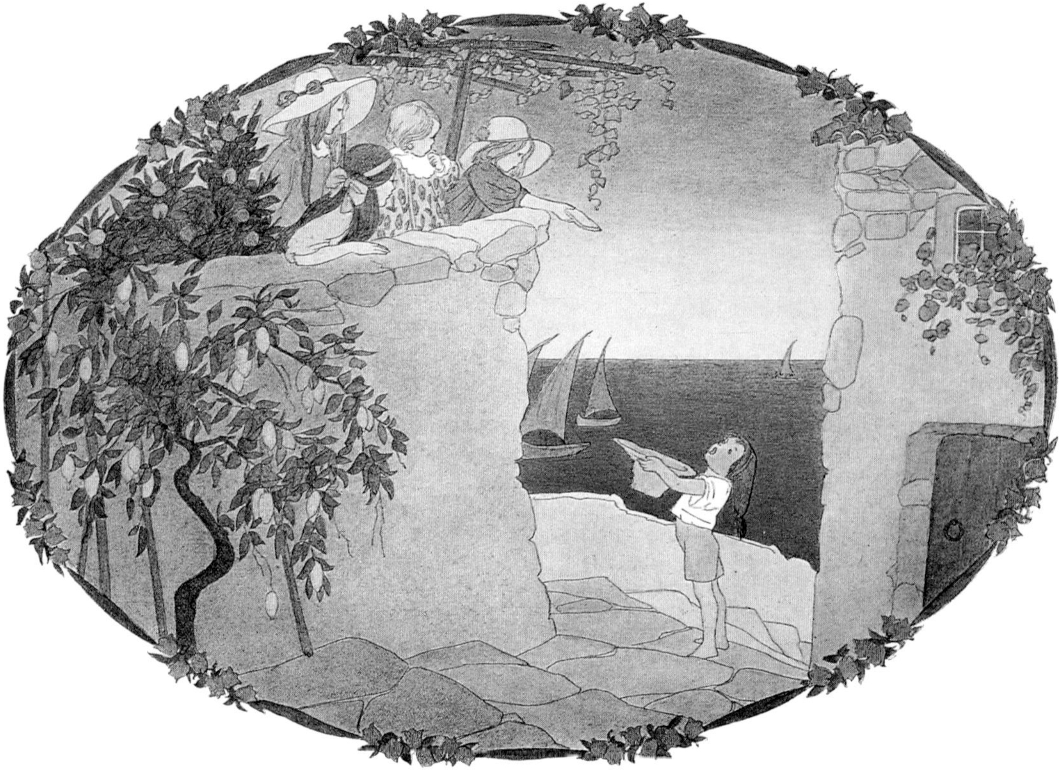

Little Tommy Tucker,
Sings for his supper:
What shall we give him?
    White bread and butter.
How shall he cut it
    Without a knife?
How will he be married
    Without a wife?

Where are you going to, my pretty maid?
    I'm going a-milking, sir, she said,
Sir, she said, sir, she said,
    I'm going a-milking, sir, she said.

May I go with you, my pretty maid?
    You're kindly welcome, sir, she said,
Sir, she said, sir, she said,
    You're kindly welcome, sir, she said.

Say, will you marry me, my pretty maid?
    Yes, if you please, kind sir, she said,
Sir, she said, sir, she said,
    Yes, if you please, kind sir, she said.

What is your father, my pretty maid?
    My father's a farmer, sir, she said,
Sir, she said, sir, she said,
    My father's a farmer, sir, she said.

What is your fortune, my pretty maid?
    My face is my fortune, sir, she said,
Sir, she said, sir, she said,
    My face is my fortune, sir, she said.

Then I can't marry you, my pretty maid.
    Nobody asked you, sir, she said,
Sir, she said, sir, she said,
    Nobody asked you, sir, she said.

23

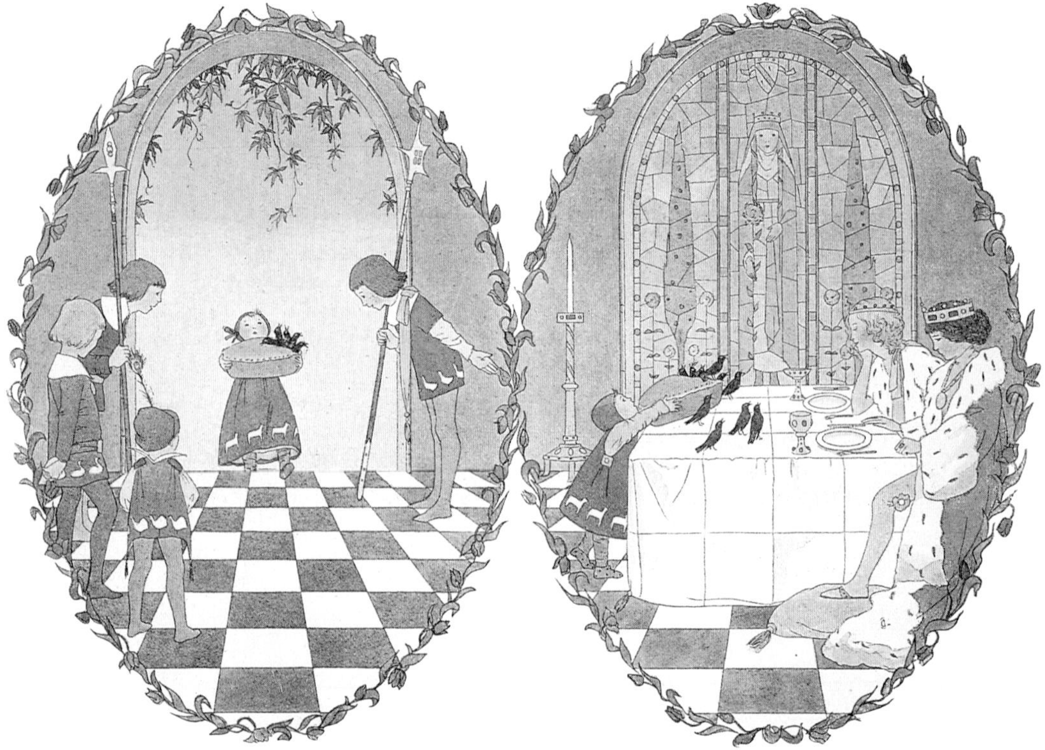

Sing a song of sixpence,
A pocket full of rye;
Four and twenty blackbirds,
Baked in a pie.

When the pie was opened,
The birds began to sing;
Was not that a dainty dish,
To set before the king?

The king was in his counting-house,
Counting out his money;
The queen was in the parlour,
Eating bread and honey.

The maid was in the garden,
Hanging out the clothes,
When down came a blackbird,
And pecked off her nose.

Oranges and lemons,
Say the bells of St. Clement's.

You owe me five farthings,
Say the bells of St. Martin's.

When will you pay me?
Say the bells of Old Bailey.

When I grow rich,
Say the bells of Shoreditch.

When will that be?
Say the bells of Stepney.

I'm sure I don't know,
Says the great bell at Bow.

Simple Simon met a pieman,
  Going to the fair;
Says Simple Simon to the pieman,
  Let me taste your ware.

Says the pieman to Simple Simon,
  Show me first your penny;
Says Simple Simon to the pieman,
  Indeed I have not any.

Simple Simon went a-fishing,
  For to catch a whale;
All the water he had got
  Was in his mother's pail.

Simple Simon went to look
  If plums grew on a thistle;
He pricked his finger very much,
  Which made poor Simon whistle.

He went to catch a dicky bird,
  And thought he could not fail;
Because he'd got a little salt,
  To put upon its tail.

He went for water with a sieve,
  But soon it all fell through;
And now poor Simple Simon
  Bids you all Adieu.

Lavender's blue, diddle, diddle,
Lavender's green;
When I am king, diddle, diddle,
You shall be queen.

Call up your men, diddle, diddle,
Set them to work,
Some to the plough, diddle, diddle,
Some to the cart.

Some to make hay, diddle, diddle,
Some to thresh corn,
Whilst you and I, diddle, diddle,
Keep ourselves warm.

Old King Cole
Was a merry old soul,
And a merry old soul was he;
    He called for his pipe,
And he called for his bowl,
And he called for his fiddlers three.

Every fiddler
    Had a very fine fiddle,
And a very fine fiddle had he;
    Oh, there's none so rare
As can compare
With King Cole and his fiddlers three.

A frog he would a-wooing go,
　Heigh-ho! says Rowley;
Whether his mother
Would let him or no,
　With a rowley, powley,
　Gammon and spinach,
Heigh-ho! says Anthony Rowley.

So off he set with his opera hat,
　Heigh-ho! says Rowley;
And on the road
He met with a rat,
　With a rowley, powley,
　Gammon and spinach,
Heigh-ho! says Anthony Rowley.

Pray, Mister Rat, will you go with me?
　Heigh-ho! says Rowley;
Kind Mistress Mousey
For to see,
　With a rowley, powley,
　Gammon and spinach,
Heigh-ho! says Anthony Rowley.

They came to the door of Mousey's Hall,
　Heigh-ho! says Rowley;
They gave a loud knock,
And they gave a loud call,
　With a rowley, powley, etc.

Pray, Missy Mouse, are you within?
　Heigh-ho! says Rowley;
Oh yes, kind sirs,
I'm sitting to spin,
　With a rowley, powley, etc.

Pray, Missy Mouse, do give us some beer,
　Heigh-ho! says Rowley;
For Froggy and I
Are fond of good cheer,
　With a rowley, powley, etc.

Pray, Mister Frog, please give us a song?
　Heigh-ho! says Rowley;
Let it be something
That's not over long,
　With a rowley, powley, etc.

But while all were a-merry-making,
　Heigh-ho! says Rowley;
A cat and her kittens
Came tumbling in
　With a rowley, powley, etc.

The cat she seized the rat by the crown,
　Heigh-ho! says Rowley;
The kittens they pulled
The little mouse down,
　With a rowley, powley, etc.

This put Mister Frog in a terrible fright,
　Heigh-ho! says Rowley;
He took up his hat and
He wished them good-night,
　With a rowley, powley, etc.

But as Froggy was crossing over a brook,
　Heigh-ho! says Rowley;
A lily-white duck came
And gobbled him up
　With a rowley, powley, etc.

So there was the end of one, two & three.
　Heigh-ho! says Rowley;
The rat, the mouse,
And the little froggy
　With a rowley, powley, etc.

Boys and girls, come out to play,
The moon doth shine as bright as day.
Leave your supper and leave your sleep,
    And join your playfellows in the street.
Come with a whoop and come with a call,
    Come with good will or not at all.
Up the ladder and down the wall,
    A half-penny loaf will serve us all;
You find milk, and I'll find flour,
    And we'll have a pudding in half an hour.

See-saw, Margery Daw,
Jacky shall have a new master;
He shall have but a penny a day,
    Because he can't work any faster.

Tom, he was a piper's son,
  He learnt to play when he was young,
And all the tune that he could play,
    Was, "Over the hills and far away";
Over the hills and a great way off,
    The wind shall blow my top-knot off.

Tom with his pipe made such a noise,
    That he pleased both the girls and boys,
And they all stopped to hear him play,
    "Over the hills and far away".
Over the hills and a great way off,
    The wind shall blow my top-knot off.

I HAD A LITTLE NUT TREE

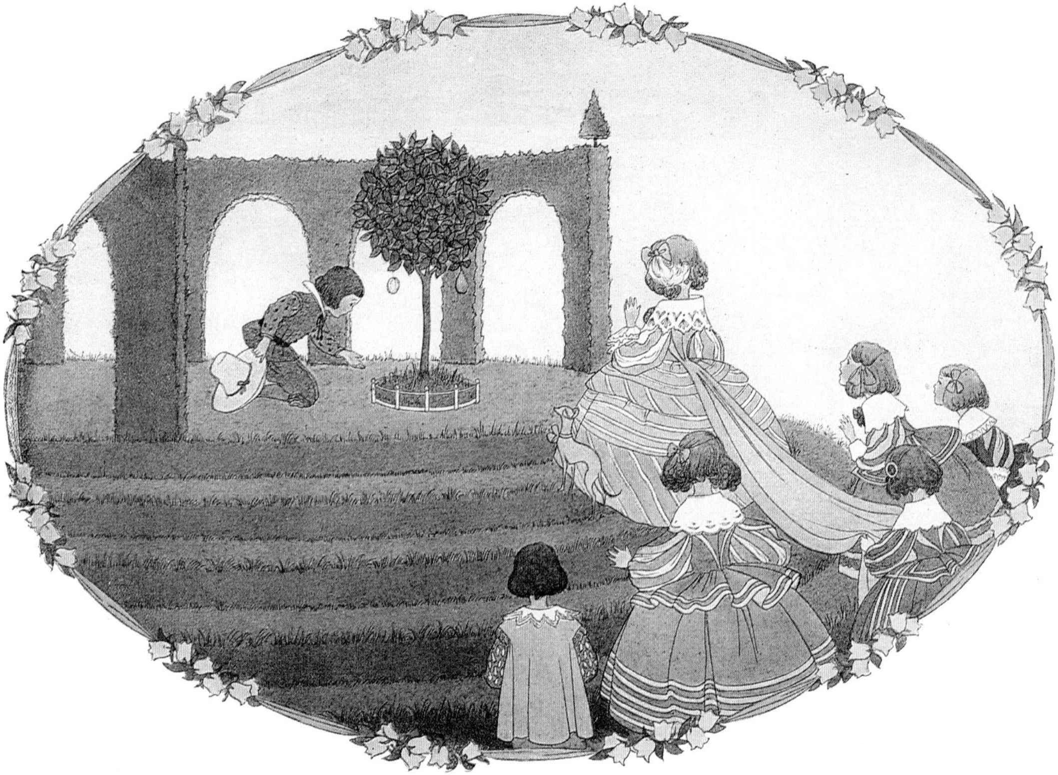

I had a little nut tree,
Nothing would it bear
But a silver nutmeg
    And a golden pear;
The King of Spain's daughter
    Came to visit me;
And all for the sake
    Of my little nut tree.

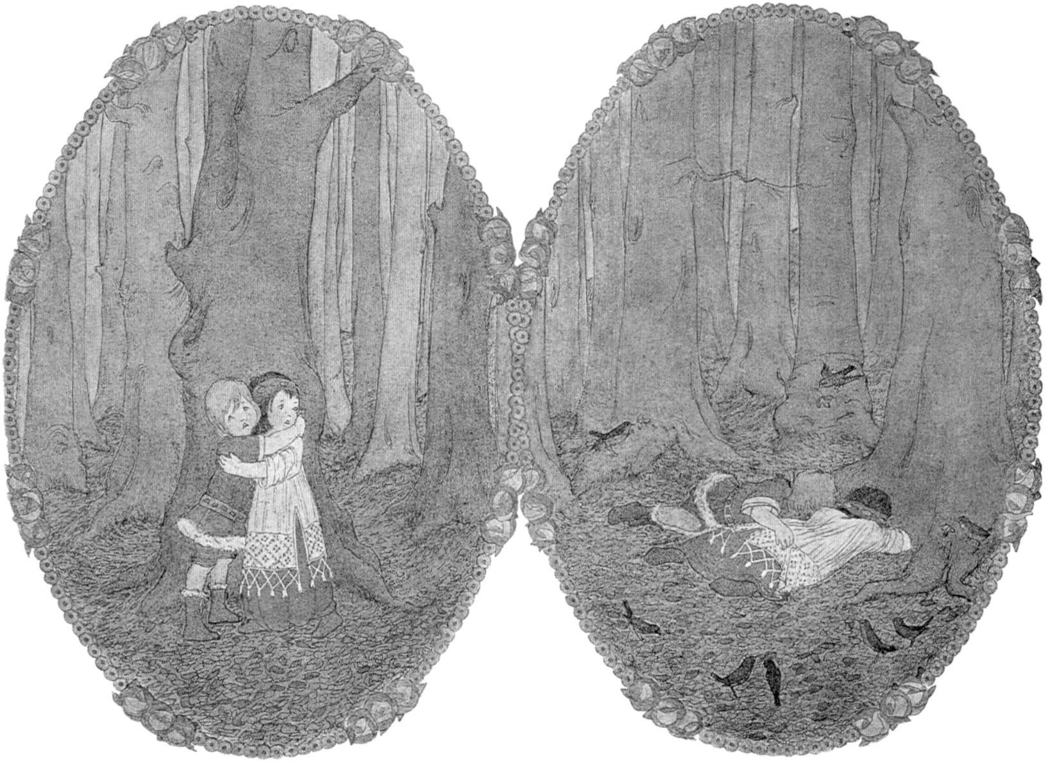

My dears, you must know,
That a long time ago,
    Two poor little children
        Whose names I don't know,
Were stolen away
On a fine summer's day,
    And left in a wood,
        As I've heard the folk say.
Poor Babes in the Wood!
Poor Babes in the Wood!
    Don't you remember
    The Babes in the Wood?

And when it was night,
So sad was their plight,
    The sun it went down,
        And the moon gave no light;
They sobb'd and they sigh'd
And they bitterly cried,
    And the poor little things
        They then lay down and died.
Poor Babes in the Wood!
Poor Babes in the Wood!
    Don't you remember
    The Babes in the Wood?

And when they were dead,
The robins so red,
    Brought strawberry leaves
        To over them spread,
Then all the day long,
The branches among,
    They mournfully whistled,
        And this was their song:
Poor Babes in the Wood!
Poor Babes in the Wood!
    Don't you remember
    The Babes in the Wood?

Twinkle, twinkle, little star,
How I wonder what you are!
Up above the world so high,
Like a diamond in the sky.

When the blazing sun is gone,
When he nothing shines upon,
Then you show your little light,
Twinkle, twinkle, all the night.

Then the traveller in the dark,
Thanks you for your tiny spark,
He could not see which way to go,
If you did not twinkle so.

In the dark blue sky you keep,
And often through my curtains peep,
For you never shut your eye,
Till the sun is in the sky.

As your bright and tiny spark,
Lights the traveller in the dark,
Though I know not what you are,
Twinkle, twinkle, little star.

47

Lazy sheep pray tell me why
In the pleasant field you lie,
Eating grass and daisies white
   From the morning till the night?
Ev'rything can something do,
   But what kind of use are you?

Nay, my little master, nay,
   Do not serve me so, I pray;
Don't you see the wool that grows
   On my back to make your clothes?
Cold, ah, very cold you'd be
   If you had not wool from me.

I SAW THREE SHIPS

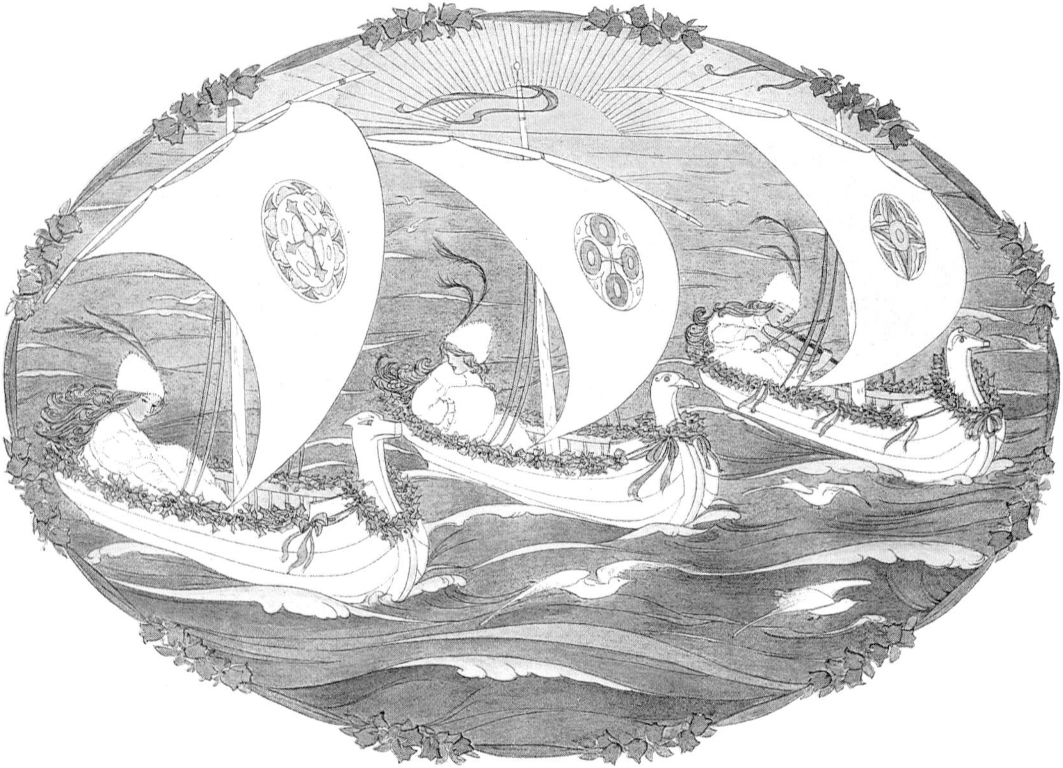

I saw three ships come sailing by,
   Come sailing by, come sailing by,
I saw three ships come sailing by,
   On New-Year's day in the morning.

And what do you think was in them then,
   Was in them then, was in them then?
And what do you think was in them then,
   On New-Year's day in the morning?

Three pretty girls were in them then,
   Were in them then, were in them then,
Three pretty girls were in them then,
   On New-Year's day in the morning.

One could whistle, and one could sing,
   And one could play on the violin;
Such joy there was at my wedding,
   On New-Year's day in the morning.

THERE WAS A CROOKED MAN

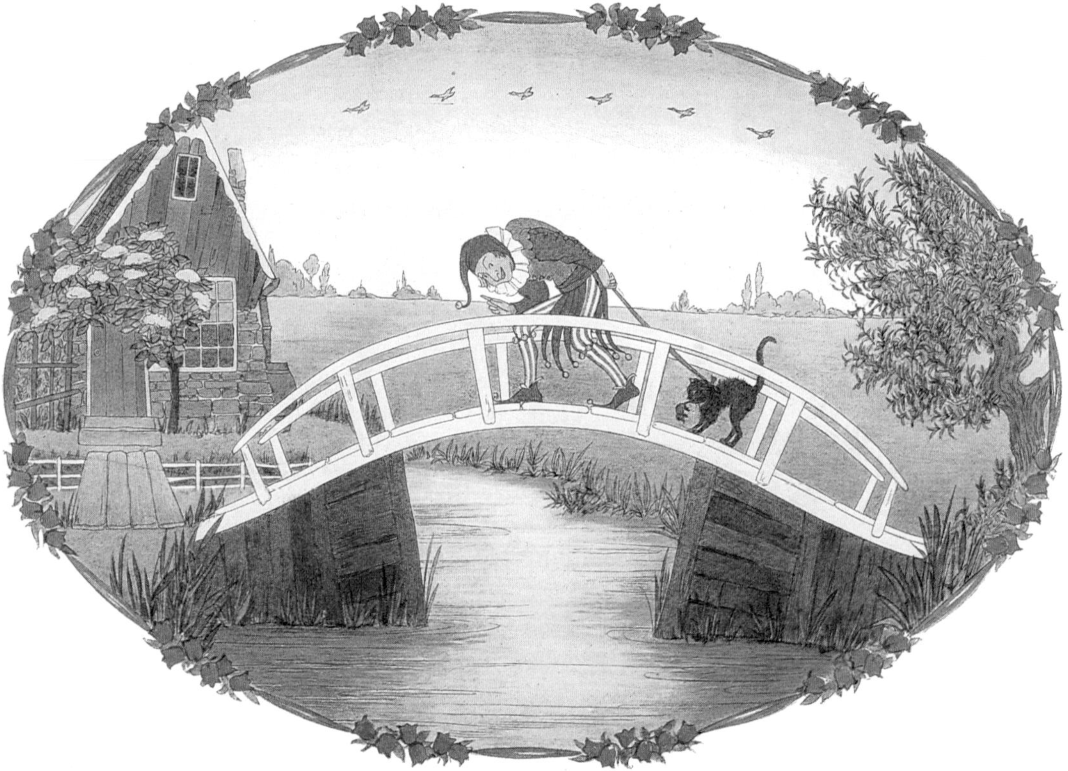

There was a crooked man,
 And he walked a crooked mile,
He found a crooked sixpence
    Against a crooked stile;
He bought a crooked cat,
    Which caught a crooked mouse,
And they all lived together
    In a little crooked house.

Four and twenty tailors
   Went to catch a snail,
The best man among them
   Durst not touch her tail;
She put out her horns
   Like a little Kyloe cow,
Run, tailors, run,
   Or she'll kill you all e'en now.

There came to my window
    One morning in spring
A sweet little robin,
    She came there to sing;
The tune that she sang
    It was prettier far
Than any I heard
    On the flute or guitar.

Her wings she was spreading
    To soar far away,
Then resting a moment
    Seem'd sweetly to say —
Oh happy, how happy
    The world seems to be,
Awake, little girl,
    And be happy with me!

Will you walk into my parlour?
　　Said the spider to the fly.
'Tis the prettiest little parlour
　　That you ever did spy;
The way into my parlour
Is up a winding stair,
　　And I have many pretty things
　　To show you when you're there.
Oh, no, no! said the little fly,
To ask me is in vain,
For who goes up your winding stair
　　Shall ne'er come down again.

The spider turned him round about
And went into his den,
　　For well he knew the silly fly
　　Would soon come back again;
So he wove a subtle web
In a little corner sly,
　　And he set his table ready,
　　To dine upon the fly:
Then he came out to his door again
And merrily did sing,
　　Come hither, hither, pretty fly,
　　With the pearl and silver wing.

Alas! alas! how very soon
This silly little fly,
　　Hearing all these flattering speeches
　　Came quickly buzzing by;
With gauzy wing she hung aloft,
Then near and nearer drew,
　　Thinking only of her crested head
　　And gold and purple hue,
Thinking only of her brilliant wings
Poor silly thing, at last
　　Up jumped the wicked spider
　　And fiercely held her fast.

59

A little cock sparrow
Sat on a green tree,
    And he chirruped, he chirruped,
    So merry was he.
A naughty boy came
With his wee bow and arrow,
    Says he, I will shoot
    This little cock sparrow;
His body will make me
A nice little stew,
    And his giblets will make me
    A little pie too.
Oh, no, said the sparrow,
I won't make a stew,
    So he flapped his wings
    And away he flew.

Sleep, baby, sleep!
Our cottage vale is deep;
The little lamb is on the green,
    With woolly fleece so soft and clean,
Sleep, baby, sleep!

Sleep, baby, sleep!
    Thy rest shall angels keep,
While on the grass the lamb shall feed,
    And never suffer want or need.
Sleep, baby, sleep!

Sleep, baby, sleep!
    Down where the woodbines creep;
Be always like the lamb so mild,
    A kind, and sweet, and gentle child.
Sleep, baby, sleep!

ILLUSTRATIONS COPYRIGHT © 1911 & 1912
BY SOEFI STICHTING INAYAT FUNDATIE SIRDAR.
TEXT COPYRIGHT © BY DAWN & PETER COPE.
PUBLISHED BY GALLERY CHILDREN'S BOOKS
AN IMPRINT OF EAST-WEST PUBLICATIONS (UK) LIMITED
NEWTON WORKS, 27/29 MACKLIN STREET,
LONDON WC2B 5LX.

ALL INQUIRIES TO EAST-WEST PUBLICATIONS.
PRINTED AND BOUND IN HONG KONG
BY SOUTH CHINA PRINTING COMPANY.
ISBN 0-85692 185 8
SECOND IMPRESSION